THE SOMERSET and DORSET JOINT RAILWAY

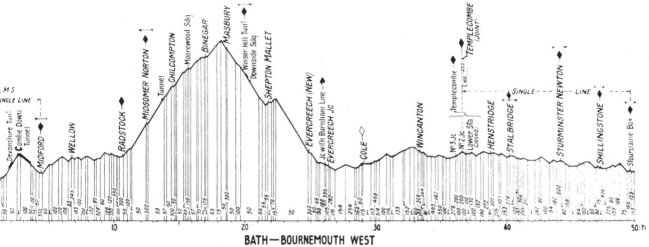

BATH—BOURNEMOUTH WEST

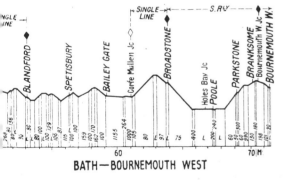

BATH—BOURNEMOUTH WEST

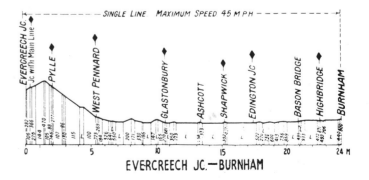

EVERCREECH JC.—BURNHAM

*gradient profiles by permission of
The Railway Magazine.*

The
SOMERSET
& DORSET
IN COLOUR

"Armstrong" 0-6-0 No. 44560 climbs towards Winsor Hill Tunnel with the 4.15pm stopping train from Templecombe to Bath. Delivered to the S&D in April 1922 as No. 60 this was one of five standard Midland Railway Class 4 0-6-0s purchased from Armstrong Whitworth & Co. Ltd. Renumbered 4560 when taken into LMS ownership in 1930, and 44560 following Nationalisation of the railways of Great Britain in 1948. This was the last of the five ex-S&D "Armstrongs" to remain in service.

19th May 1962

The End of an Era

Some of the residents of Midsomer Norton turn out to witness the passing of the last "Pines Express" to travel via the S&D on the final day of summer Saturday through express workings over the line. BR Class 9F, 2-10-0 No. 92220 *Evening Star*, in the capable hands of Driver Peter Guy and Fireman Ron Hyde (the latter seen looking out from the cab of the locomotive), storms up through Midsomer Norton station. Never again would enthusiasts be able to witness the exciting spectacle of the "Pines" and other through trains battling over the steep Mendip gradients between Bath and Evercreech Junction.

8th September 1962

Through traffic from the Midlands had been a feature over the S&D since the opening of the Bath to Evercreech extension in 1874, and such workings soon developed to include destinations from the North of England. Commencing on 1st October 1910, a through train ran as a daily restaurant car express from Manchester to Bournemouth, a service which – in 1927 – acquired the title the "Pines Express". Unlike all other express trains using the line, the "Pines" ran, Mondays to Saturdays, throughout the year to become the S&D's 'premier train'. It was the re-routeing of the "Pines Express" in 1962, to run via Oxford and Basingstoke which, together with the withdrawal of all of the summer Saturday through trains, was to herald the 'death knell' of the Somerset & Dorset.

THE **NORMAN LOCKETT** COLLECTION

The
SOMERSET
& DORSET
IN COLOUR

Mike Arlett & David Lockett

BCA

LONDON · NEW YORK · SYDNEY · TORONTO

The Somerset & Dorset in Summer . . .
A heat haze hangs over the beautiful Midford Valley as 2P class 4-4-0 No. 40564 and a modified SR
Pacific (probably No. 34028 *Eddystone*) speed southwards with the 'down' "Pines Express".

This edition published 1991 by BCA by arrangement with Oxford Publishing Co., Sparkford, near Yeovil, Somerset
BA22 7JJ.

CN1542

Printed by: J. H. Haynes & Co. Ltd
Typeset in Times Roman Medium 10/11pt.

Introduction

Those of you who have seen (and hopefully purchased!) a copy of *The Norman Lockett Collection – Great Western Steam in the West Country* may have noticed that David Lockett and myself had intended the next volume published to feature *Southern Steam – South & West*. Indeed, preparations were well in hand when, in the late-summer of 1990, the realisation suddenly 'hit' me that 1991 would mark the twenty-fifth anniversary of the closure of the 'Somerset & Dorset' line.

Over a period of many years, it has become apparent to my wife, Sandra, that the suggestion of the occasional summer evening 'excursion' is the precursor to visiting, for example, some remote bridge spanning an overgrown cutting in the Mendip Hills. Luckily, Sandra's 'sense of direction' has never proved one of her stronger points, but she is, however, sufficiently versed in 'matters S&D' to realise that a roadside sign indicating say, Shepton Mallet, is but a few miles distant, means we are heading to view "the remains" of yet another derelict section of what was my favourite railway line! This, inevitably, leads to such utterances as, "oh, not again" (or worse!) so I have, therefore taken to 'subterfuge', travelling via country lanes where signposts are few and far between. On one such trip, during August 1990, I had succeeded in getting to within but a few miles of my 'goal' without my wife realising as to where we were heading. The delightful village of Batcombe was to prove my downfall; had Sandra noticed that half-hidden roadsign indicating *'Evercreech 2'* ? Her next enquiry confirmed the worst – "And when did *you* last have occasion to drive this way?" Well, on counting back, it was "more than thirty years ago"; and it was undertaken by bicycle – a fifty mile round journey to visit Evercreech Junction one summer Saturday in the late 1950s.

Could it really have been that long ago? Never did that old adage, *"doesn't time fly"* appear more appropriate. But *"yes"*, it must be, for my eldest daughter, Sarah, was born in 1966, and she will be 25 next birthday. And, that's how and when I suddenly realised the impending 'anniversary' of closure of the S&D!

As I have previously recalled, in the 'Introduction' to *Great Western Steam in the West Country,* it was Ivo Peters who urged me to see the photographs taken by his late friend. This finally proved possible in 1988 when, having 'tracked down' Norman Lockett's son, David, I was able to view the superb collection. What I had not appreciated, from Ivo, was the wealth of colour material, in the format of 35mm transparencies. Those of you who are aware of my affinity to the S&D will well imagine my reaction on viewing a collection which includes more than 250 'slides' featuring just this line alone. What was needed was a 'justification' for publishing some of this material – and what better an excuse than to choose the year coinciding with the twenty-fifth anniversary of the closure of the line!

The period from 1958 to 1966, when Norman Lockett photographed the S&D in colour, includes of course those years which witnessed the sad decline and closure of the line. In the late fifties, however, little other than rumour indicated the impending fate of the S&D. Despite the fact that the summer Saturday 'peaks' of through traffic had started to

. . . The Somerset & Dorset in Winter
S&D 7F class 2-8-0 No. 53809 standing just north of Binegar station with the rear portion of a 'down' freight which had been retrieved after being stuck fast for several days in a deep snow drift.
Sunday 6th January 1963

decline, it was still an exciting period for the enthusiast who was able to witness the greatest variety of motive power ever to be seen working over the Mendip Hills. Whilst classes new to the S&D were introduced – the BR 'Standards', modified Bulleid Pacifics and ex-Great Western locomotives – it was still possible to see those types of motive power traditionally associated with the S&D. At least, that was the position until early in 1962, which marked the demise of the ever-faithful ex-LMS Class 2P 4-4-0s. To my mind, above all else, it was the loss of these marvellous old engines (which had spent their last year on piloting duties during the summer of 1961) which marked the *beginning of the end* of the S&D that I knew, and wish to recall, during the post-war era.

One problem in producing this book has been the identification of details of some of the trains and locomotives featured. Unlike the black and white negatives, which were recorded in great detail by Norman Lockett, few such details were recorded of his colour transparencies. However, in the knowledge that many of Norman's lineside visits were made in the company of Ivo Peters, I have been able to turn to Ivo's notes and albums to track down many of the details and dates. Similarly, the wealth of material published by the S&DR Trust, in the bi-monthly *'Bulletin',* has yielded the answer to many queries. Where, however, uncertainty has remained, I have not sought to assume the details; knowing only too well from previous experience that any date or detail incorrectly 'guessed at' will, inevitably, bring forth retribution!

This book takes the now traditional format of a journey from Bath to Bournemouth. There is just one difference; *it's all in colour!*. Like most others who photographed the S&D, Norman found the greatest interest on the northern section between Bath and Evercreech Junction. This book reflects that bias but, even so, there are more than forty photographs which feature the line south of 'the Junction.' As regards 'the Branch'; by the date when Norman Lockett began to pay the occasional visit to photograph, in colour, the line from Evercreech to Highbridge, the train services were all but the exclusive domain of the ex-GW Collett 0-6-0s. Such motive power, to my mind, was not representative of the 'Branch' in the manner in which I would wish it to be recalled! Coverage of this section, the original main line of the Somerset Central Railway, is restricted, therefore, to include (in addition to just one or two of the latter-day service trains) some of the 'specials' which traversed the Somerset Levels in the final years before closure, behind motive power more often associated with the pre-1960 era.

David Lockett and myself hope that this 'all-colour' trip down the line will rekindle happy memories for those who made such journeys – or visited the lineside at some favourite location – in the 1950s and early-60s. For those too young to recall such an experience, it is a colour portrait of what you have missed!

Mike Arlett
North Bradley
Wilts

Notes
Train times are quoted from the Working Time Tables.
(SO) after a train time indicates that the service ran on Saturdays Only during the summer period.
Bridge Numbers and names are taken from the official S&D Bridge List.
A number of photographs in this album have been reproduced from original colour transparencies which, although not of the best exposure quality or colour rendering, have been included because of their historical interest. The slow exposure speed of colour film of approximately thirty years ago also made it difficult to 'freeze' a fast moving train in dull conditions. However, it was considered that the rarity of such illustrations in colour made them worthy of inclusion.

Bath Green Park

My earliest memories of 'Green Park' date from the start of the 1950s. Frequent all-day shopping excursions to Bath with my parents enabled me to 'escape' for lengthy visits to the 'Midland Station'. I still recall vividly the involuntary quickening of pace on turning into James Street West, where the distant frontage of Green Park came into view. Little could I have imagined then that 25 years later I would, in my capacity of Principal Building Surveyor with Bath City Council, be clambering over the roof of the same station, now derelict and awaiting what seemed inevitable demolition. Neither could I have envisaged that a few years later, I would be witnessing the wonderful restoration of the same building and giving a talk on the history of the station in the superb 'Meeting Room' which has been formed above what was, until 1966, the 'Booking Hall'.

Back in the early-1950s, the only part of that elegant façade of interest to me was the open pair of entrance doors leading into the Booking Hall, beyond which might be seen – through another pair of open doors – the outline of an ex-LMS locomotive. At Green Park, unlike the 'Western' station, you didn't even have to purchase a penny platform ticket to 'watch the trains'. Occasionally, I was able (with parental permission) to travel down the line as far as Radstock. The price for a 'child return' must have been about one and sixpence ($7\frac{1}{2}$p); the equivalent of three weeks' pocket money in those days!

Through the pages of this book, thanks to the pictures of Norman Lockett, we can 'travel' the S&D again and witness many of the sights which had for so long been taken for granted but were soon to disappear for ever. So join David Lockett and myself on this journey of memories down the line to Bournemouth.

Many commentators give the impression that Green Park was a hive of activity. Certainly this was so on busy summer Saturdays, but at other times the visitor would be more likely to witness lengthy periods of inactivity, punctuated by brief interludes of bustling action; not least the daily (Sundays excepted) comings and goings of the "Pines Express". This picture, therefore, depicts Green Park as many may recall it best; with a semi-fast train waiting to depart for Bournemouth from the southern (No. 1) platform. The column of steam seen at the rear end of train reveals that this is a through service from Bristol, Temple Meads. BR Standard Class 5 4-6-0 No. 73050 had been allocated, brand new, to the S&D in June 1954. Here, the locomotive's livery is a sad reflection of the immaculate condition witnessed nine years previously, when No. 73050 arrived at Bath motive power depot immediately following public display at the International Railway Congress Association Exhibition at Willesdon. Today it can be seen on the Nene Valley Railway at Peterborough.

24th September 1963

Bath Green Park

Right, top: BR Class 9F No. 92220 *Evening Star* had been transferred to Bath for a brief period during 1962, in order to haul the final workings of the "Pines Express" to run via the S&D line. In the summer of 1963 the locomotive was again transferred to Bath mpd; this time to cover for a temporary shortage of motive power. But with heavy passenger traffic no longer running over the line, *Evening Star* spent this further sojourn on the S&D working three and four coach stopping trains. Here, she waits to depart from Bath with one such service; the 1.10pm to Templecombe.

12th September 1963

Right, below: Over a period of many years, pigeon traffic was a regular feature over the S&D, with Templecombe a favourite release-point for birds sent by the Federations based in the Midlands and the North of England. With a rush of steam from the cylinder cocks, Stanier Class 8F 2-8-0 No. 48737 sets off from the northern (No. 2) platform at Green Park with a pigeon special bound for the Lower Yard at Templecombe.

17th August 1963

From the 1950s, the Ian Allan organisation ran several enthusiasts' specials over the S&D. One such trip, in September 1962, was hauled by S&D Class 7F No. 53808; the special being taken over at Bath by an ex-GWR 'Hall' for the run over to Bristol on the journey back to London. Having completed her duties, No. 53808 has been turned, and runs forward past Stanier Class 8F No. 48660 prior to setting back into the S&D shed.

22nd September 1962

Bath Motive Power Depot

A sad occasion. No. 53807, the last of the class to remain in service, had been withdrawn from traffic the previous day. The 7F is seen here standing ahead of an ex-LMS Stanier locomotive which had suffered a similar fate. To the left is the 60 ft diameter turntable and, beyond, the rear of the larger S&D running shed can be seen.

6th September 1964

Left: "Jinty" 0-6-0T No. 47506 stands outside the old Midland Railway shed, in company with more modern motive power. The Type 4 diesel, No. D44 was, at the time, based at Derby shed, and had worked down to Bath with a parcels train from the North. The stone-built two-road shed dated from 1870, having been brought into use shortly after the opening of the MR line from Mangotsfield on 4th August 1869.

12th February 1964

The S&D Motive Power Depot

Right, top: On the same occasion as featured on page 10, No. 53808 has retired to the S&D shed, and to the company of two other 7Fs: No. 53806 (behind), and No. 53807 – the latter standing on the *'Boat Road'*, left. This gave access to the riverside line and the sidings which served the large engineering works of Messrs Stothert & Pitt. Also in view, an ex-LMS Stanier and, to the right, BR Class 3MT 2-6-2T No. 82004. The S&D shed, of timber and asbestos construction, dated from 1874/5. Originally a two-road shed, this was enlarged to four roads in 1878 and extended forward in 1884.

22nd September 1962

A 9F on Trial. An evocative scene which rekindles the atmosphere of Bath motive power depot. BR Class 9F 2-10-0 No. 92204 waits in the rain beside the coaling stage, prior to working a test train over the S&D. This was to assess the capability of these engines to haul, unassisted, the heavy passenger traffic which ran over the line. In charge of No. 92204 and the test train was my good friend Driver Bill Rawles, together with Fireman Ronald Bean. Despite appalling weather on the day, the test proved a complete success, and led to the transfer of four of the 'Class Nines' to Bath for the duration of the summer services from 1960 until 1962.

29 March 1960

Previous pages: Closure of the S&D had been announced to take effect on 3rd January 1966, but almost at the last moment one of the operators authorised to provide one of the replacement bus services withdrew his application for an operating licence. The Western Region of BR, unable to make alternative arrangements within the available time, was forced to delay closure of the line until 6th March 1966. On what was meant to be a last day working, the RCTS ran a special from Bournemouth Central to Bath, hauled by SR Class U 2-6-0 No. 31639 and 'West Country' class Pacific No. 34015 *Exmouth*. After the run up to Bath, the locomotives were photographed 'on shed'. Having been turned and reunited, the locomotives stand in the wintry sunlight alongside the rear of the brick-built coaling stage.

2nd January 1966

Below: A view taken from the coaling stage, looking towards the connection with the main line, seen in the distance. The motive power on view (on what appears to be an official 'shed visit') includes BR Class 4 2-6-0 No. 76062, a Stanier 'Jubilee' 4-6-0 and a Class 4F 0-6-0. BR Class 5 No. 73050 is standing on 'No. 8 Road', which ran to the rear of the tall water softening plant; from the top of which Ivo Peters obtained his superb 'bird's-eye view' photographs of the mpd. The circular bases, seen to the right, are a reminder of the abortive government-inspired post-war scheme to convert a large number of the nation's steam locomotives to oil firing. These concrete circles formed the bases to the two oil storage tanks, which although erected, were destined never to be used.

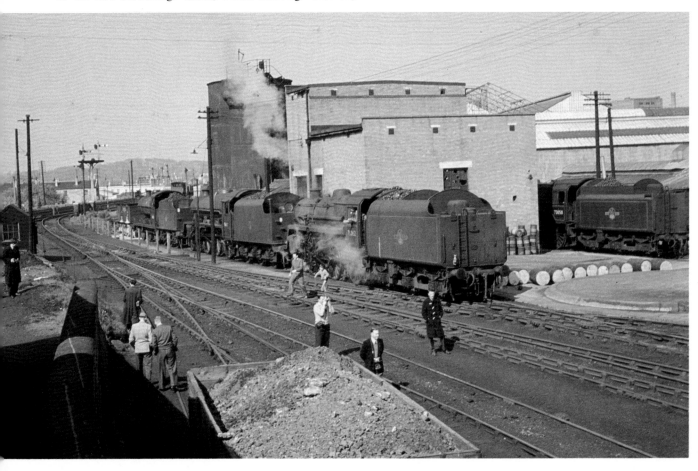

Bath – Departure and Arrival

BR Class 5 No. 73049 sets off with a train for Templecombe. The start was made from the north platform at Green Park (platform No. 2), and the train is about to cross over onto the correct running line to Bath Junction. Stanier Class 8F No. 48660 is standing on the line serving the brick-built coal stage; the latter dating from 1954 as the replacement of an earlier timber structure built in 1874/5.

22nd September 1962

Another BR Class 5, No. 73012, joins the Midland line at Bath Junction with the 9.05am from Templecombe; passing ex-GWR 0-6-0 pannier tank No. 3742 engaged on shunting duties. In the background is the signal box which controlled the junction with the S&D single-line section to Midford.

25th September 1963

Devonshire Bank. From Bath Junction, the S&D single line to Midford commenced on a wide sweeping turn, climbing at a gradient of 1 in 50. Following the briefest of level sections, where a siding served the Co-op bakery, climbing recommenced – first at 1 in 66, before steepening again to 1 in 50 for a hard slog up the long straight which led into Devonshire Tunnel. At Maple Grove, a three-arch footbridge spanned the line, providing a wonderful 'vantage point' from which to watch the heavy passenger and freight trains ascending the bank. A classic S&D motive power combination from the 1950s; Class 2P 4-4-0 No. 40563 and SR Pacific No. 34040 *Crewkerne*, the latter still in original condition, climb towards Devonshire Tunnel with the 6.57am (SO) Cleethorpes to Bournemouth.
Summer 1959

Overleaf: In 1960, after a lapse of many years, the destination of the summer Saturdays' service from Cleethorpes reverted from Bournemouth to Exmouth. Leaving the S&D at Templecombe, the train ran over the SR Salisbury – Exeter main line to Sidmouth Junction and thence, via Tipton St Johns, to Exmouth. A corresponding service ran in the reverse direction. The 'down' train is seen here, climbing out of Bath behind ex-S&D Class 4F 0-6-0 No. 44558, assisted by BR Class 4 4-6-0 No. 75009.
11th August 1962

Requiring no assistance, BR Class 9F 2-10-0 No. 92233 passes under the Maple Grove overbridge (Bridge No. 9) and climbs through the cutting leading to Devonshire Tunnel, with the 7.43am (SO) Bradford to Bournemouth West.

August 1962

Right, top: Emerging out of the tunnel into the sunshine, BR Class 5 No. 73049 and SR Pacific No. 34043 *Combe Martin* coast down the 1 in 50 bank towards Bath with the 12.20pm (SO) Bournemouth to Nottingham.

18th August 1962

Right, below: S&D Class 7F No. 53807 emerges from Devonshire Tunnel and plods up through Lyncombe Vale with a train of coal empties bound for Norton Hill Colliery.

October 1962

Devonshire Tunnel

Lyncombe Vale

After emerging from the ¼ mile long Devonshire Tunnel, the single line continued at 1 in 50 through Lyncombe Vale, to reach the summit of climb out of Bath just a few yards before entering the northern portal of Combe Down Tunnel.

Left, top: BR Class 4 4-6-0 No. 75027 climbs through Lyncombe Vale with the 1.10pm local from Bath to Templecombe . . .

Left, below: . . . and heads across Watery Bottom Viaduct and into the tree-lined cutting leading up towards the summit of the climb at Combe Down Tunnel. This locomotive is now based on the Bluebell Railway.

25th September 1962

Caught in the rays of the early evening sun, BR Class 5 No. 73047 climbs through Horsecombe Vale, towards Combe Down Tunnel, with the 3.40pm Bournemouth West to Bristol, Temple Meads. The train has just crossed Tucking Mill Viaduct, at the near side of which can be seen (above the rear carriage) the Midford 'down distant' signal.

Early August 1963

North of Midford

After the passage of Combe Down Tunnel, one could not have wished for a better contrast than that presented from the train on the run down towards Midford station; the single line emerging from the tunnel to cross the wooded Horsecombe Vale on a splendid viaduct before descending past the grounds of Midford Castle.

Overleaf: On a lovely bright morning, S&D Class 7F No. 53807 heads south, tender-first, past the grounds of Midford Castle with a train of coal empties bound for the Norton Hill Colliery at Midsomer Norton. Note, that despite the train running on a down-grade, the locomotive has 'steam on', and the guard will have the brake to his van screwed down hard; both in accordance with working instructions to keep all couplings taught. This served to prevent a 'snatch', and the possibility of a broken coupling when the train reached the upgrade to the south of Midford station.

24th September 1963

Midford: The Long Arch Bridge

BR Class 5 No. 73047 emerges from the 37-yard long tunnel (No. 17 – 'The Long Arch Bridge') and coasts down towards Midford station with the 9.30am Whit Sunday excursion from Bath to Bournemouth. Note the pouch, containing the single-line tablet, in position for automatic collection by the lineside catcher opposite Midford signal box. The profusion of wild flowers on the lineside cutting adds to the delights of the beautiful countryside to be seen along this section of the S&D line.

21st May 1961

Midford Station

BR Class 4 2-6-0 No. 76015, with the 12.55pm Bournemouth West to Bristol, Temple Meads, collects the tablet for the single line section to Bath Junction. To the left is the 'down starting' signal – a tubular post with lower quadrant arm provided by the Western Region as the replacement for the earlier signal, the wooden post of which had developed a noticeable 'sway' whenever the upper quadrant arm was 'pulled off'! The oil lamp, at the entrance to the small Waiting Room/Booking Hall survived until closure of the line.

27th June 1964

Overleaf: **'Home from Home'** Reminiscent of my first view of the Somerset & Dorset when, in June 1952, I 'discovered' the line here at Midford. This was the view from the south end of the station platform; the signal box where I spent so very many happy hours. The crew of Class 2P 4-4-0 No. 40697 check that the single line tablet is out for collection by Bulleid Pacific No. 34040 *Crewkerne*, as the passage of the 'up' ''Pines Express'' rattles the windows of the signal box. Unlike the station, somewhat belatedly (in 1958) the box gained the advantage of electric lighting, although, like Midford signalman Percy Savage, I much preferred the warm glow of the old oil lamps!

The impressive and unusual combination of a Stanier 'Black Five', No. 44867, and modified SR Pacific No. 34029 *Lundy,* pass onto the single line section whilst crossing Midford Viaduct with the 12.20pm (SO) Bournemouth to Nottingham.

4th August 1962

This delightful late-afternoon view, taken from Primrose Hill, shows BR Class 4 4-6-0 No. 75027 and modified SR Pacific No. 34029 *Lundy* with the 10.55am (SO) Manchester to Bournemouth West, which was scheduled to pass Midford at 4.31pm.

4th August 1962

Midford Viaduct

The four mile single-line section from Bath Junction ended at Midford; double track being regained on the viaduct (situated immediately to the south of the station) and extending for 32 miles until reaching Templecombe No. 2 Junction. Midford Viaduct, 168 yards long and built with eight arches, carried the S&D over the main road, the remains of the Somersetshire Coal Canal, the GWR Limpley Stoke to Camerton branch line and Midford Brook.

The doyen of the BR 'Class Nines': No. 92000 heads southwards onto double track with the 7.45am (SO) Bradford to Bournemouth, passing the 'up inner home' signal. No. 92000 was one of four 'Class Nines' allocated to the S&D for the 1961 summer services. Midford Castle can be seen on the skyline nestling amongst the trees.

8th July 1961

Viewed from the derelict trackbed of the old GWR Limpley Stoke – Camerton branch line, BR Class 5 No. 73049 approaches Midford Viaduct in the early evening sunshine, with the 3.40pm from Bournemouth. The steep lane known as Primrose Hill, which led to Twinhoe – and provided a gated access to the Midford 'up' siding – is to the right of the lineside embankment.

4th July 1962

Midford

No. 75072, one of the double-chimney BR Class 4 4-6-0s, sets off from Midford, and commences to climb the 1 in 60 gradient towards Lower Twinhoe, with the 3.20pm 'down' local from Bath to Templecombe.

27th June 1964

A Bath to Templecombe stopping train, hauled by ex-LMS Class 4F 0-6-0 No. 44417, pulls away from Midford with the usual 3-coach green-liveried Maunsell set strengthened with a coach in contrasting BR 'crimson lake and cream' livery. A swathe of grass has been scythed down adjacent to the lineside, but the remainder remains uncut and is brightened by a fine display of buttercups.

Another dramatic view. BR Class 4 No. 75072, assisting an unidentified BR Class 5 with the 'down' "Pines Express", passes the 'Midford B' ground frame which controlled access to the Up siding. The ground frame points were released by lever No. 11 in Midford signal box. The siding and ground frame were taken out of use around November 1959, and removed shortly thereafter.

I have to admit to a certain bias, but there can be few with memories of the S&D who will argue that this was amongst the finest of lineside locations. (For me, it was *the* finest, and so it will come as no surprise that this is my favourite picture!)

Class 2P 4-4-0 No. 40652 and a BR Class 5 regain double track, and are about to 'open up' as they head 'No. M245' – the 7.40am (SO) Bradford to Bournemouth – up the 1 in 60 gradient towards Wellow. The date was unrecorded, but No. 40652 transferred to the S&D in May 1959, whilst the 'up' siding and ground frame are yet to be removed. The date must therefore be during the summer of 1959.

Between Midford and Wellow

Class 2P 4-4-0 No. 40697 threads through the countryside near Wellow with a 'down' stopping train from Bath to Templecombe. I wonder if a running fault resulted in the removal of one of the Maunsell coaches from the usual 3-coach set, and the replacement by the ex-LNER Gresley brake composite?
16th April 1960

Left, top: Driver Donald Beale gives a cheery wave to Norman Lockett and Ivo Peters as modified SR Pacific No. 34047 *Callington* sweeps through the cutting, passing the tall 'down advanced starting' signal, with the 10.20am (SO) Liverpool to Bournemouth.
11th June 1960

Left, below: The afternoon calm in the Wellow Valley is disturbed briefly by Class 2P 4-4-0 No. 40563 and a BR Class 9F (which I believe may be No. 92205), as they head the 10.28am (SO) Manchester to Bournemouth past Lower Twinhoe and the Midford 'up distant' signal, approximately mid-way between Midford and Wellow.
Summer 1960

South of Midford. BR Class 4 No. 75023, and green-liveried BR Class 5 No. 73054, swing through the reverse curves towards Lower Twinhoe with the 'down' "Pines Express". In the background, is the Midford 'up outer home' signal. This was the point where, on summer Saturdays, many an 'up' express was brought to an involuntary halt, awaiting clearance of the single-line section before proceeding into Bath.

26th May 1962

BR Class 5 No. 73047 heads towards Midford with an 'up' express. Although not readily apparent from this view, the train is crossing Wellow Viaduct, situated immediately beyond the linesman's hut seen at the far end of the cutting. Beyond the viaduct, the line curves out of view on the approach to Wellow station.

August 1960

Wellow

The village of Wellow is approached by narrow lanes with gradients of a severity which were sufficient to deter the ambitions of local bus operators until the 1960s. The picturesque station, conveniently close to the village centre, therefore remained well patronised right up to the closure of the Somerset & Dorset in March 1966.

Right, top: S&D Class 2-8-0 No. 53801 heads north-east away from Wellow with an 'up' goods train. This view is as seen from an occupation overbridge (which we always knew locally as the "Blue Bridge") and which provided a pleasant backdrop of Wellow village, including the tower of St Julian's church.

25th March 1961

Right, below: Heading away from Wellow towards Radstock, one of several excursions which ran over the S&D in the line's latter years and which utilised diesel multiple units – a form of motive power never seen in regular traffic.

Many readers may know that in 1959 Ivo Peters wrote to the General Manager of the Western Region of BR, suggesting the use of the Class 9F 2-10-0s for working, single-handed, the heavy summer expresses which ran over the S&D. Not only did Ivo receive a long letter of reply but, the following year, four of the "Nines" were allocated to Bath. What is not generally known however, is that in 1965 Ivo wrote again to BR suggesting that the S&D might be 'saved' if economies could be attained by singling much of the line, and introducing dmus for passenger, and Brush Type 4 diesels for freight traffic. This time, sadly (but perhaps not surprisingly), Ivo received no reply!

With the Wellow 'up distant' signal showing 'all clear', BR Class 9F 2-10-0 No. 92000 hurries by with the 3.35pm semi-fast from Bournemouth. The depression to the right of the line is the bed of the 'Radstock arm' of the old Somersetshire Coal Canal, later converted to a tramway, the course of which – following purchase by the S&D – was utilised as much as possible for construction of the line between Radstock and Midford.

15th August 1961

Wellow to Shoscombe

Running fast around the reverse curves north-east of Shoscombe & Single Hill Halt, BR Class 5 No. 73052 swings under the road bridge, near Stoney Littleton, with an 'up' express.

Left: By far the best way to enjoy the delightful countryside to be seen from the carriage window was to travel on one of the local stopping trains; the leisurely progress providing ample opportunity to 'take in' the scenery. A Class 4F 0-6-0 ambles round the curve south of Wellow village, which can be seen in the right background, and heads towards Stoney Littleton.

18th June 1960

Radstock

Beyond Shoscombe the scenery changed dramatically, as the S&D approached Radstock, 10½ miles south-west of Bath. Here was the centre of the Somerset Coalfield which, with many of the collieries connected to the S&D, provided the railway with an important source of traffic for ninety years.

Left top: The view of Radstock Yard, as seen by members of the Bath Railway Society from the brake van of a 'down' freight. "Jinty" 0-6-0T No. 47557 waits to run forward to provide banking assistance to Masbury Summit. In the left background is Radstock 'A' signal box and, to the right, the motive power depot (a sub-depot to Bath) which housed the small stud of locomotives used for shunting and banking duties.

24th September 1963

Making a cautious approach to Radstock with the 6.25am freight from Evercreech Junction to Bath, S&D Class 7F No. 53808 crosses the bridge carrying the line over the route of the old Welton Tramway.
27th September 1963

The Climb out of Radstock

From Radstock station, the Somerset & Dorset commenced a $7\frac{1}{2}$ mile climb towards the summit of the line, high in the Mendip Hills, near Masbury.

Left, below: Commencing the long climb from Radstock, S&D Class 7F No. 53804 heads a Sunday excursion organised by the Stephenson Locomotive Society. On the far right is the single-line ex-GWR 'North Somerset' branch line from Frome to Bristol, over which the S&D crossed on the North Somerset Viaduct – better known locally as the 'Five Arches'.

11th September 1960

Climbing the 1 in 50 towards Midsomer Norton, Class 2P 4-4-0 No. 40700 and BR Class 5 No. 73050 are in charge of a Whit Sunday excursion from Cheltenham to Bournemouth. The scenery in this view, south of the 'Five Arches' is somewhat deceptive, giving no indication of what is to follow within the next half mile – a massive 'dirt batch' (the waste from Norton Hill Colliery)!

21st May 1961

Norton Hill Colliery

Just before reaching Midsomer Norton station, the S&D connected, on the 'down' side, with the large colliery at Norton Hill, where the National Coal Board used one of their own locomotives for shunting the colliery yard.

Left, top: No. 53809 comes up the long stretch of 1 in 50 towards Midsomer Norton, passing the connection leading to the colliery sidings. At the rear of the freight a plume of smoke reveals the presence of the banker providing valuable rear-end assistance.

5th October 1963

Left, below: Following the sad demise of the famous S&D Class 7F 2-8-0s, the last of which, No. 53807, was withdrawn from service in September 1964, coal traffic from Norton Hill was entrusted to the ex-LMS Stanier Class 8F 2-8-0s. No. 48760 reverses a train of empty wagons into the colliery sidings whilst the NCB locomotive, a Hunslet 0-4-0T (builder's No. 1684), pauses between shunting duties. The latter survives today and is currently on the Swanage Railway.

5th October 1965

High above the town of Midsomer Norton, No. 53809 is featured again, keeping company with Class 3F 0-6-0T No. 47496 at the entrance to the colliery. Despite a programme of comprehensive modernisation works to Norton Hill as late as 1960, the planned efficiences were, allegedly, unachieved and the colliery closed in mid-February 1966, just a few weeks before the shut-down of the S&D. No. 53809 has, of course, suffered a kinder fate. Rescued from Barry scrapyard and restored to full working order by the late Frank Beaumont, the locomotive is now based at the Midland Railway Centre at Butterley, and is passed for main line running on BR.

27th September 1963

Overleaf: **Steam and snow at Midsomer Norton.** Class 3F 0-6-0T No. 47496, fitted with a snow plough and assisted by Stanier Class 8F No. 48660, about to set off 'wrong line' in what was to prove a successful attempt to clear the 'up' line from Binegar. Earlier, the 'down' line had been cleared as far south as Winsor Hill, and S&D Class 7F No. 53809 is waiting to head off to retrieve the rear portion of the previous Thursday's 3.30pm 'down' freight, which was being 'dug out' of a deep snow drift.

6th January 1963

Midsomer Norton

The delightful station at Midsomer Norton is, perhaps, best remembered for the wonderful floral displays which reflected the pride – and much hard work – of the staff; attributes which typified very many who worked on the S&D.

With some of the floral display in view BR Standard Class 5 No. 73051 blasts through the station with the 9.30am (Sundays) Bristol, Temple Meads to Bournemouth.

6th August 1961

Right, top: Ex-GWR 0-6-0 No. 2291, in charge of a short 'up' freight, is brought to a halt to enable the driver to speak with the signalman at Midsomer Norton. Just peeping into view, on the extreme right is the lean-to greenhouse in which, each year, the station staff raised the bedding plants for the summer floral displays.

28th September 1963

The Climb to Chilcompton Tunnel

Passing through the station at Midsomer Norton, the gradient eased to 1 in 300, but immediately beyond the platform end climbing recommenced in earnest.

BR Class 4 4-6-0 No. 75023 and modified Bulleid Pacific No. 34039 *Boscastle* attack the 1 in 53 gradient just beyond Midsomer Norton station, with the 'down' "Pines Express". Notice the excellent condition of the permanent way and, in the background, how the 'up home' signal is provided with a white sighting board which enabled the signal arm to be seen more easily against the otherwise dark backcloth of the trees. *Boscastle* is now the subject of a restoration project on the Great Central Railway.
14th July 1962

Just back from an overhaul at Eastleigh Works, and resplendent in a fully lined green livery, BR Class 5 No. 73049 bursts out of Chilcompton Tunnel on a dull rainy morning with the 9.55am, semi-fast service from Bath to Bournemouth.

5th October 1963

Chilcompton Tunnel

Left, top: A 9F shows its true worth: No. 92206, with twelve on, climbs the long hard slog at 1 in 53 from Midsomer Norton, with the 10.20am (SO) Manchester to Bournemouth. Here, at the end of a long straight (well, 'long' by S&D standards!), the line curves into a rock cutting leading to Chilcompton Tunnel.

9th July 1960

Left, below: Another locomotive destined to escape the cutter's torch. BR Class 4 4-6-0 No. 75027 assists SR Pacific No. 34041 *Wilton* to make a vigorous ascent towards the tunnel with the 10.38am (SO) Manchester to Bournemouth.

9th July 1960

Overleaf: Class 2P 4-4-0 No. 40569 assists a BR Class 5 4-6-0 to lift the Saturdays only Bradford to Bournemouth through the 66-yard long Chilcompton Tunnel, to emerge into the sunlight on a lovely summer day. Note how each line passes through a separate bore; a reminder that the S&D was, original-ly, extended from Evercreech to Bath as a single line. The train is passing through the original tunnel, dating from the opening of the 'Bath Extension' in 1874, whilst the separate tunnel serving the 'up' line dates from 1886, when the section between Radstock and Binegar was doubled.

South of Chilcompton Tunnel

No. 53808 propels an engineer's train 'wrong-line' up the gradient, immediately south of the tunnel. The leading brake van is approaching the point where the gradient eased, albeit only very briefly, before climbing onwards – now at 1 in 50 – into the rock cutting which led towards Chilcompton station.
September 1960

Left, below: S&D 7F No. 53807 pounds up the final few yards leading to Redan Bridge (Bridge No. 51) and into the rock cutting at Chilcompton, with the 8.55am Bath to Evercreech Junction freight. The twin portals of Chilcompton Tunnel may just be seen in the left background.
28th September 1963

As at Midsomer Norton, the gradient through Chilcompton station was eased to 1 in 330, but see how the line reverted to 1 in 50 immediately beyond the platform. BR Class 4 2-6-0 No. 76006 restarts the 1.10pm from Bournemouth; a service for which the SR provided the motive power. Whilst never allocated to the S&D, the BR Standard Class 4 2-6-0s were regular performers over the line from 1955.

14th September 1963

Chilcompton to Moorewood

From Chilcompton station, the climb towards Masbury Summit continued on a ruling gradient of 1 in 50 as far as Old Down, on the approach to Moorewood. Here the grades eased, although there was still another $2\frac{1}{2}$ miles of climbing to face, on gradients as steep as 1 in 63.

Right, top: As the result of Sunday occupation of the 'down' line for engineering work, near Moorewood, the SLS Special (featured earlier leaving Radstock) is halted at Chilcompton and set back onto the 'up' line. The pilotman, identified by his red armband, supervises the points being clipped before authorising the driver of S&D 7F No. 53804 to proceed 'wrong line' to Binegar, where the train would recross to the correct running line.

11th September 1960

Right, below: The view from the guard's van of a Bath to Evercreech Junction freight train, climbing past the Moorewood 'down distant' signal on the approach to Old Down, about one mile south of Chilcompton.

24th September 1963

A Whit Sunday excursion from Bristol to Bournemouth, hauled by 2P Class 4-4-0 No. 40697 and BR Class 5 No. 73019, climbs south from Burnt House Bridge (Bridge No. 57), where the gradient levelled briefly on the approach to Moorewood Sidings.

21st May 1961

On a lovely sunny morning, an S&D Class 7F drifts down the bank from Binegar with a freight from Evercreech Junction to Bath. How much better the old style 'Somerset County Council' signpost fitted into the countryside compared with the large metal roadsigns in use today.

27th September 1963

Right, top: BR Class 9F No. 92233 with an August Bank Holiday excursion – the 8.50am from Bath to Bournemouth – climbs past Portway Bridge, about ¾ mile north-east of Binegar. The weather appears all too typical of a bank holiday (proving that some things never change!).

6th August 1962

Between Moorewood and Binegar

Right, below: Despite this being a rare combination of motive power (even by S&D standards!), it's amazing how many people captured this event on film. But I believe this to be the first time it has been published in colour. Ex-GWR Collett 0-6-0 No. 3215 and Bulleid Pacific No. 34043 *Combe Martin* run down towards Moorewood signal box with the 12.20pm (SO) Bournemouth to Nottingham.

8th September 1962

The "Pines Express" climbs past the Binegar 'down distant' signal, behind Class 2P 4-4-0 No. 40563 assisting modified SR Pacific No. 34046 *Braunton*. On the left is the Moorewood 'up distant'; an old LSWR-pattern lower quadrant signal arm attached to a lattice post. In contrast, the Binegar 'distant' comprises an SR upper quadrant arm with two lengths of rail bolted together to form the post.

Drawing near to Binegar, an ex-LMS Class 4F 0-6-0 No. 44422, built at Derby in 1927, crosses Tillet's Lane Bridge with the 3.20pm stopping train from Bath to Templecombe. No. 44422 was destined for preservation by the North Staffordshire Railway at Cheddleton.

14th September 1963

Contrasts at Binegar

As New Year 1963 was heralded in, the West Country was swept by blizzards. Strong winds whipped the heavy blanket of snow into huge drifts. Some of the worst conditions were experienced high on the Mendips and, despite heroic efforts by staff, the S&D succumbed to the weather on Thursday 3rd January. On the following Sunday, Norman Lockett accompanied Ivo Peters to Midsomer Norton and Binegar to record the efforts to clear the line.

Right, top: At Binegar station, the snow had piled up between the platforms and had first to be dug out the 'hard way', before it was safe to allow the plough engine and the assisting Stanier 8F to proceed with their efforts to clear the line southwards. Despite the arctic conditions, note that the windows in the signal box were open; they were a hardy breed on the S&D!

6th January 1963

Right, below: No. 53807 pauses at the south end of the station. All those who recall the 'good old days' (the era of steam and the S&D), should consider how the gentleman on 'snow duty' must have been feeling! No doubt, the station-master's house, seen to the right, would prove a welcome haven, especially if Mrs Down had the kettle on the boil.

6th January 1963

With evidence of hay-making in full swing, BR Class 4 No. 75027 provides valuable assistance to modified SR Pacific No. 34042 *Dorchester*, as they storm up the final few yards of the climb towards Bridge No. 69 (Oakhill Road Bridge) and the summit of the line, with the 10.38am (SO) Manchester to Bournemouth.

8th July 1961

Just over the top at Masbury; S&D Class 7F No. 53808 heads the Locomotive Club of Great Britain special, "The Somerset & Dorset Rail Tour", down the bank towards Binegar Bottom.

30th September 1962

Masbury Summit

From Binegar, southbound trains faced a final mile of climbing before reaching the summit of the line, in a rock cutting 811 feet above sea level.

Right, top: S&D Class 7F No. 53808 heads another enthusiasts' special; this time organised by Ian Allan Ltd. Breasting the summit, a short level section (which extended just 120 feet) preceded the point reached here by No. 53808, which marked the start of the long descent towards Radstock.

22nd September 1962

Right, below: No. 53807 nears the end of the climb with the 8.55am freight to Evercreech Junction. From Radstock, the train has been assisted at the rear, and here at the summit the 'banker', a Class 3F 0-6-0 "Jinty" tank, will drop off to return 'wrong line' to Binegar.

28th September 1963

With a surplus of steam, BR Class 4 4-6-0 No. 75073 drifts down the 1 in 50 gradient from the summit, and approaches Masbury Halt with a local service from Bath to Templecombe.

Early May 1962

Masbury

The late-afternoon sunshine highlights the 3.40pm from Bournemouth to Bristol, with BR Class 9F No. 92220 *Evening Star* climbing the 1 in 50 past the Masbury 'up distant' signal.

17th August 1962

Memories of happy days at Winsor Hill. A pair of BR Standard 4-6-0s, Class 4 No. 75023 and Class 5 No. 73054 with the 'down' "Pines Express", emerging at speed from Winsor Hill Tunnel, and heading down the long straight towards Shepton Mallet.

26th May 1962

Winsor Hill

A sad picture taken only a few days before closure of the line, during the period when the Western Region of BR – having failed to secure the S&D's fate on 3rd January 1966 (the original date set for closure) – was forced to provide an 'emergency service' until alternative arrangements could be finalised, thus permitting the 'axe to fall' on Sunday, 6th March 1966. An unidentified BR Class 4 2-6-0, climbs towards Winsor Hill Tunnel.

26th February 1966

Entering Shepton Mallet. The descent from Masbury Summit to Evercreech Junction was interrupted, albeit for less than a mile, at Shepton Mallet. The break in the down-grade occurred half-way across the impressive 27-arch Charlton Road Viaduct. The viaduct, curving high above the town outskirts, can be seen in the background of this view, as ex-S&D Class 4F 0-6-0 No. 44560 approaches Shepton Mallet (Charlton Road) station with the 3.20pm 'down' local from Bath.

7th September 1963

Shepton Mallet in the Rain

A reminder that, even in summer, the sun did not always shine on the S&D!

Class 2P 4-4-0 No. 40564 and BR Class 5 No. 73051, with the 'up' "Pines Express" pass the goods shed and cattle pens, immediately to the south of the station.

1st April 1961

Right, top: The 'up' "Pines" is featured again as, in the midst of a heavy downpour, the train slows to a halt behind BR Class 4 4-6-0 No. 75023 and modified SR Pacific No. 34046 *Braunton*. The attractive signal box at Charlton Road was 'pure S&D', but note that the influence of the Western extends not only to the station seat, but also the livery of the second coach of the "Pines". Somehow, "chocolate and cream" always looked very out of place on the 'Dorset'!

6th August 1962

Right, below: After a one-minute pause, the "Pines" sets off again, and in such conditions both engine crews were, no doubt, wishing to take full advantage of the brief downhill start before tackling the arduous climb ahead towards Winsor Hill and Masbury Summit.

6th August 1962

A Stanier 8F on passenger work. No. 48309 pauses at Shepton Mallet with the 1.10pm 'down' local from Bath. Ivo Peters (who undoubtedly, would have christened this picture "the biter bit!") hurries away from the platform to obtain a further 'shot' of No. 48309 setting off, for the continuation of the run down to Templecombe.

9th October 1965

Shepton Mallet (Charlton Road)

No. 53807 in charge of the 8.55am Bath to Evercreech Junction freight, has been set back into the 'down' yard to clear the main line for a following passenger train. As with most 'down' freight trains, water was taken at Shepton Mallet.

28th September 1963

On an overcast morning, 2P class 4-4-0 No. 40569 and modified SR Pacific No. 34039 *Boscastle* climb through the cutting near Cannard's Grave with the 9.25am (SO) Bournemouth to Manchester. The lineside post indicates the mileage (22) from Bath Junction.

25th June 1960

South of Shepton Mallet

Climbing away from Shepton Mallet, and passing under the GW line from Witham to Yatton, the S&D recommenced the southern descent of the Mendips towards Evercreech Junction. Near Cannard's Grave, the line entered a long cutting which, within the mile, was spanned by no less than six overbridges.

On the last Saturday before closure, the Locomotive Club of Great Britain ran a 'Farewell Special' over the line. Seen here, climbing northwards from Prestleigh Viaduct towards Shepton Mallet, the special is hauled by two SR Bulleid Pacifics – "West Country" No. 34006 *Bude* and "Battle of Britain" No. 34057 *Biggin Hill*. Both locomotives were turned out in immaculate external condition and, working in tandem, provided a vivid reminder of happier days from the 1950s.

5th March 1966

The combination of a blue sky and brilliant sunshine provides the impression of a lovely autumnal day, but look how the near-vertical exhaust of hard-working No. 53808 is snatched away by the strong wind. The 7F presents a stirring sight as it passes northwards over Prestleigh Viaduct with the LCGB "Somerset & Dorset Rail Tour".

30th September 1962

This fine panoramic view of the viaduct shows the last-ever pairing of two ex-S&D locomotives. The train, a special organized by the Home Counties Railway Society, was worked over the line by 7F class 2-8-0 No. 53807 (ex-S&D No. 87 of 1925) piloting 4F class 0-6-0 No. 44558 (ex-S&D No. 58 of 1922).

7th June 1964

Prestleigh Viaduct

About 1½ miles south of Shepton Mallet the line passed over Prestleigh Viaduct (Bridge No. 95). Like all other viaducts on the Bath to Evercreech section of the S&D, this structure, comprising eleven arches, was built originally to accommodate only a single line. The viaduct was widened when the line between Shepton Mallet and Evercreech New was 'doubled' in 1888, and still stands today.

Left, below: Another view taken from the guard's van, as a Stanier Class 8F eases a 'down' freight over the viaduct, on the 1 in 50 descent towards Evercreech.

24th September 1963

Near Evercreech New

About half a mile north of Evercreech New, No. 92220 *Evening Star* with the 3.40pm 'up' from Bournemouth, passes over Bridge No. 99 (known as Evercreech Road Bridge). This was the longest unbroken stretch of 1 in 50 on the entire line, extending 2½ miles from Evercreech New station to the summit at Cannard's Grave.

1st September 1962

Ex-S&D Class 4F 0-6-0 No. 44559 coasts in with a Bath to Templecombe local. As at many other stations on the 'Bath Extension', the ruling gradient was eased to 1 in 300 for the passage through the station at Evercreech New.

7th July 1962

Evercreech New

The opening of the Evercreech to Bath extension in 1874 enabled the S&D to provide a station immediately adjacent to the village. The original station – now renamed Evercreech Junction – lay some two miles to the south.

Right, top: The view from the signal box steps, as BR Class 4 2-6-0 No. 76019 approaches the station with the 1.08pm (SO) Bournemouth to Bristol. Consider the workmanship which must have gone into producing that delightful platform lamp; so different – and so much more pleasing – than the modern lamp-posts provided today.

7th July 1962

Right, below: From the field to the west of the line, BR Class 5 No. 73054 comes up the bank with a Sunday train from Bournemouth, reaching the point where the 1 in 50 gradient eased for the passage through the station which, incidentally, was known for the first two months following opening in 1874, as Evercreech Village.

8th September 1962

This is one of my favourite pictures, and makes me wish I had visited the attractive station at Ever-creech New more often than proved possible in the days before I owned my first car. Even on a rainy day, the sight of a northbound express hammering up through the station was a rousing sight.

Such is seen here, with Class 2P No. 40569 assisting a modified Bulleid Pacific. The signal box, it will be noted, is not of the usual design being the result of a fire which destroyed the original box, and led to this replacement which dated from 1920. *1st April 1961*

Evercreech Junction North

Contrary to popular belief, the line southwards from Evercreech New did *not* fall all the way to the Junction. At Pecking Mill, where the S&D crossed the A371 road, the long descent was interrupted first by a brief level section, followed by a *rising* gradient and another short level. Thereafter, the descent was resumed through a sharply curved cutting to join the route of the line from Highbridge.

Left, top: Ex-GWR Collett 0-6-0 No. 3218 drifts past the North Box at Evercreech Junction, with the afternoon milk train from Bason Bridge to Templecombe. The 'Branch' – the original main line of the Somerset Central Railway – can be seen running straight into the distance, whereas the 'extension' line to Bath turned away north-eastwards on a severe curve. On the right of this view is one of the distinctive 'wrong road' (also referred to as 'calling back' or 'backing') signals. This signal authorised a freight train, upon arrival from the Bath line, to reverse on to the 'down' line and then onto the 'Branch', from where it could be propelled into the once busy Up Yard.

25th July 1964

Left, below: **Great Western Takeover!** Ex-GWR 0-6-0 No. 2219 coasts down the approach to Evercreech Junction, with a train from Highbridge, passing 'sister' No. 3210 which has paused between shunting duties in the Up Yard. Until the late-1950s, the yards at Evercreech were always busy, with shunting and remarshalling of wagons taking place 'around the clock'; many of the heavy freights departing northwards to Bath requiring the assistance of a banking engine.

20th April 1963

Below: The 7am (SO) Cleethorpes to Exmouth train, hauled by BR Class 4 4-6-0 No. 75009 and an unidentified Class 4F 0-6-0, slows to call at the 'Junction'. Generally, the assisting engine would be taken off the train at Evercreech Junction, but on this particular service, the pilot sometimes worked through as far as Templecombe station, where the train was handed over to SR motive power.

August 1962

Left, top: BR Class 4 2-6-0 No. 76015 sets off in the rain with the 1.10pm from Bournemouth to Bath. As noted earlier, the motive power rostered for this service was provided by the Southern Region; the return working being the 7.05pm Bath to Bournemouth. No. 76015 was, at this date, allocated to Bournemouth Central mpd.

20th April 1963

Evercreech Junction

Left, below: No. 75071, one of the BR Class 4 4-6-0s fitted with a double-chimney, pulls away with a Bournemouth to Bath train. The small station yard and goods shed can be seen in the centre background.

24th September 1963

No. 53808 (looking in *nearly* as good condition as it would 29 years after Norman Lockett took this photograph!), stands in the station yard, waiting to take over the LCGB "Somerset & Dorset Rail Tour", which has featured already in earlier pages. Now owned by the S&DR Trust, No. 53808 has been restored to full working order. Today, it operates between Minehead and Bishop's Lydiard, on the West Somerset Railway, where the S&DR Trust has its headquarters based at Washford.

30th September 1962

BR Class 5 No. 73054 pauses at Evercreech Junction during the run down to Templecombe with the 1.10pm local from Bath. Just a few years previously, a summer Saturday would have witnessed the siding between the two running lines full of engines, waiting to assist the heavy northbound through trains over the Mendips to Bath. But at least some things didn't change; the station-master's house (to the right) still exhibited the usual annual show of geraniums!

3rd August 1964

A BR Class 9F on Trial

Left, top: In weather not really akin to colour photography (but too interesting an event to miss!), BR Class 9F 2-10-0 No. 92204 calls at Evercreech Junction to take on water. This was the 'down' run of the trial to assess the capability of the BR 'Nines' for working heavy summer Saturday trains, unassisted, over the S&D.

Left, below: The return run sees No. 92204 halted, again to take on water, before setting off on the final leg of the run back to Bath. By now, the weather had deteriorated even more, but despite such adverse conditions, the trial proved a success. As the result, four of the 9F class Standards were to be allocated to Bath each summer from 1960 to 1962.

29th March 1960

The view southwards from the station footbridge at Evercreech Junction on a sunny summer afternoon. Gone are the steep gradients encountered on the climb over the Mendips; now the railway would pursue a far more gentle course, although the changes in gradient would remain just as frequent! BR Class 4 2-6-0 No. 76027 reaches the level crossing at the end of the long straight leading up from Wyke Champflower. To the right, the tall South Box controlling the level crossing with the A371. Also prominent is the large water tower: a necessity bearing in mind that most trains called at the Junction to enable locomotives to take on water.

25th July 1964

Setting off from Evercreech Junction

No. 73054, with Donald Beale and Peter Smith in charge, sets off from the Junction with the 'down' "Pines". Obviously, Peter has built up a good head of steam during the pause at the station! In the left background, the local 'hostelry', the Railway Hotel which, following closure of the S&D was renamed The Silent Whistle. As memories of the S&D recede into history, the owners again saw fit to change the name, this time to The Natterjack. A great pity when you consider the former importance and continuing 'fame' of Evercreech Junction, and surely a loss of commercial potential!

Right, top: BR Class 4 2-6-4T No. 80013, with a Bath to Templecombe train, passes under Bridge No. 115 (known in the official S&D Bridge List as 'Wyke Champflower Bridge'). The bridge is of interest, being the only stone-built overbridge on the S&D to span both tracks with a single arch – an indication that it was built *after* this section of the line was 'doubled' in 1884.

3rd July 1965

Wyke Champflower

Two miles south from Evercreech Junction, and having crossed two minor roads on the level at Lamyatt and Bruton Road Crossings, the railway skirted the hamlet of Wyke Champflower. Here, in 1862, the Somerset Central Railway, extending southwards from Glastonbury, met 'end-on' with the Dorset Central Railway, coming northwards from Templecombe. In the same year, these two companies were amalgamated to form the Somerset & Dorset Railway. With completion of the line between Templecombe and Blandford in 1863, a through route was created from the Bristol Channel at Burnham, to Wimborne and – via the LSWR route – to the South Coast at Hamworthy, near Poole.

Right, below: Our old friend, the LCGB "Somerset & Dorset Rail Tour" is featured again, this time passing Wyke Champflower on the run up the main line from Broadstone to Evercreech, where No. 53808 took a rest while the special ran along the branch to Highbridge and back.

30th September 1962

Ivatt Class 2 2-6-2T No. 41307, with an afternoon 'up' local from Templecombe, runs northwards through the picturesque surrounds leading towards Bridge No. 115. To the rear of the train, where the line is seen curving sharply to the east, is the spot generally regarded as the 'meeting point' between

the Somerset Central and Dorset Central Railways. Here, also, is the point where a spur was constructed to a proposed junction with the Wilts, Somerset & Weymouth line, west of Bruton.

Cole

Beyond 'Wyke Curve', the S&D turned southwards again, crossing the Great Western West of England main line. Then followed a five arch viaduct before the S&D reached Cole; the most northerly station built by the Dorset Central Railway.

On a sunny spring afternoon, ex-S&D 4F 0-6-0 No. 44560 – old No. 60 built by Armstrong Whitworth & Co. for the S&D in 1922 – climbs over Cole Viaduct with the 4.15pm 'up' local from Templecombe to Bath.

14th April 1962

Left: With the 'up starting' signal showing "all clear", No. 44102 – one of the Class 4F 0-6-0s built by Kerr, Stuart & Co. in 1925/6 – awaits the guard's whistle, before setting off with the 4.15pm 'up' local from Templecombe. Cole Viaduct can just be seen in the background; visible between the two platform lamps on the left.

8th September 1962

Right: Although the architectural style of Cole station was very different to the stations encountered thus far on the journey down the line from Bath, there was one theme of consistency – the pride taken by the staff with the platform gardens. (Perhaps, however, a little 'over-enthusiasm' with the whitewash brush!) The station nameboard reads "Cole for Bruton"; the latter a small town a mile to the northeast, and served from the station as early as 1876 by a horse-drawn omnibus.

Class 2P 4-4-0 No. 40696 sets off from Cole with a Bath to Templecombe train. As with the architectural style of the station, so too the appearance of the signal box was very different to that seen north of Cole. Coincidentally, the station was to become a 'frontier point' once again when, in 1950, the boundary between the Western and Southern Regions of the recently-created British Railways was drawn across the S&D at Cole. Later still, the influence of the 'Western' was to extend even further southwards; but as far as I recall that Region's 'house colours' – of chocolate and cream – were never to 'deface' the paintwork of any S&D station beyond Cole.

1959

Left, top: Another Class 4F, No. 44422, pulls away from Cole with the 4.13pm local from Evercreech Junction to Templecombe. This was the service which, until 1962, provided a connection at Evercreech with the 'down' "Pines Express", and called at Cole, Wincanton and Templecombe. With the "Pines" no longer running via the S&D, this was (as author Robin Atthill recalls in his classic history of the line) one of those "utterly meaningless connections which continued to feed non-existent passengers into" (and in this instance, from) "a ghost "Pines"."

17th August 1963

Left, below: BR Class 4 4-6-0 No. 75072 emerges from under Pitcombe Road Bridge (Bridge No. 121, just south of Cole station) with the 4.15pm 'up' local from Templecombe. On the skyline, in the left background, one of the several private boarding schools to be found at Bruton, which provided considerable 'start and end of term' traffic at Cole station until the very last years of the S&D remaining open.

17th August 1963

Near Shepton Montague

I always considered the stretch of line beyond Cole, passing the hamlets of Pitcombe and then Shepton Montague, to be extremely picturesque. After the deep cutting south of Bridge No. 121, the line ran on an embankment with fine views of the countryside before reaching the rock cutting, and the appropriately named high-arched overbridge – Rock Cutting Bridge – some $2\frac{1}{2}$ miles north of Wincanton.

Ex-GWR Collett 0-6-0 No. 3206 heads southwards, into the rock cutting, with the afternoon perishables "train" from Highbridge to Templecombe. Little wonder that the service proved unremunerative in the latter years, after the 'Western' had diverted milk traffic via their own main line from Highbridge.

7th July 1962

Nearing Rock Cutting Bridge

The 'down' "Pines Express" runs round the curve and into the rock cutting behind modified Bulleid Pacific No. 34042 *Dorchester*. Just before reaching the cutting passengers obtained a distant view of Redlynch House, set in the wooded grounds a mile or so to the east of the line. Another $2\frac{1}{2}$ miles of running brought the S&D through Wincanton and on towards the once-important railway 'crossroads' at Templecombe.

7th July 1962

Templecombe No. 2 Junction

Right, top: Approaching Templecombe No. 2 Junction from the north, the 'road' is set for BR Class 5 No. 73019 and train to run on to the single line to Blandford; this service not scheduled to call at Templecombe station.

August 1960

Right, below: BR Class 5 No. 73087 *Linette*, in charge of a northbound train, sweeps up the last few yards of a single-line section from Blandford Forum. The spur leading from No. 2 Junction, and climbing towards the Upper station at Templecombe, can be seen behind the rear of the train.

August 1961

In the early-afternoon of a splendid summer day, S&D Class 7F No. 53810 runs up the spur leading to the SR station at Templecombe with the 7.35am (SO) Nottingham (Midland) to Bournemouth West. The roof of the motive power depot can be seen to the right of the line.

A sad occasion: Ivatt 2-6-2T No. 41249 has been coupled to the rear of a last day special and pulls out from Templecombe station to draw the train down the connecting spur to No. 2 Junction.

6th March 1966

Contrasts at Templecombe

A happier era – yet only $7\frac{1}{2}$ years prior to the date of the previous photograph – SR Bulleid Pacific No. 34062 *17 Squadron,* slows to a halt at Templecombe with an Exeter to Waterloo express. No. 34062 was rebuilt about six months later, but survived in modified form only a further five years, being withdrawn from traffic in June 1964. In the right background, the carriages of a through S&D train, which used the outer face of the 'up' island platform.

Summer 1958

S&D 7F No. 53807 runs up the grade towards Templecombe No. 2 Junction, returning 'light engine' to Bath. Note the pouch containing the single-line tablet, set up ready for collection by the lineside automatic 'catcher' at Templecombe No. 2 Junction signal box, which can be seen in the distance. On the right, the once-busy Lower Yard, which also gave access to the motive power depot.

11th August 1962

In order to avoid a separate 'light engine working' from Bath to Bournemouth (and, more important-ly, to ensure that fireman Peter Smith gets home in time for an evening out with his fiancée!), Bulleid Pacific No. 34043 *Combe Martin* has been coupled ahead of BR Class 9F No. 92245 with the 7.43am (SO) Bradford to Bournemouth. Having called first at Templecombe Upper, the train has been hauled back to No. 2 Junction, and now sets off southwards again, heading down the single line section towards Stalbridge.

11th August 1962

Left, top: No. 40564 – the second of the LMS Fowler locomotives built in 1928 as a development of the Midland Railway Class 2P, was allocated to the S&D in December 1947. It remained on the line until withdrawal from service at Templecombe in February 1962. The vehicle in red livery on the far right was of LSWR origin, and had been converted for use as a Mess & Tool coach. Also seen in the background is the former goods shed, to the rear of which ran the original spur leading to the LSWR main line. After removal of the connection with the main line in 1870, this spur was cut back to serve as a siding. Prominent in the foreground is the 50 ft diameter turntable – just too short for turning the S&D Class 7F 2-8-0s.

11th September 1960

Left, below: At the head of this line-up is Stanier Class 3MT 2-6-2T No. 40171; one of four such locomotives allocated to Templecombe in 1960. The clean appearance belied a poor mechanical condition, which resulted in only the briefest period of use on the S&D. Behind the Stanier tank is Class 2P 4-4-0 No. 40634, built at Derby by the Midland Railway. As No. 45 it was one of three such locomotives supplied new to the S&D in 1928, arriving on the line resplendent in the famous Prussian blue livery adopted by the railway in 1886. The slate-roofed building seen behind No. 40171, was the original Dorset Central Railway station dating from 1862, and used as such until closure in 1887, after which the building was converted for use as offices for the motive power depot.

11th September 1960

Templecombe Motive Power Depot

Motive power depot facilities at Templecombe dated back to 1863. In 1877 an enlarged two-road timber built shed was brought into use as a replacement for the original building. This later structure survived (just!) until 1951, when the Southern Region of BR erected a new running shed, constructed in brick with an asbestos-sheeted roof.

Stabled in the siding between the single line to Stalbridge and the brick-built running shed is "Bulldog" 0-6-0 No. 43194 and "Jinty" Class 3F 0-6-0T No. 47542. Built by the Midland Railway, and delivered new to the S&D as No. 62 in January 1896, No. 43194 nears the end of a long career, being withdrawn from service at Templecombe just three months after being photographed here by Norman Lockett.

11th September 1960

On a glorious sunny afternoon. No. 53804 – one of the original S&D Class 7Fs built by the Midland Railway in 1914 – sets off down the single line from No. 2 Junction, with the 9.10am (SO) Birmingham to Bournemouth. After passing the mpd, the single line ran under the SR Salisbury-Exeter main line, to which the S&D was connected by the spur to the left, climbing from No. 2 Junction to the Upper station at Templecombe.

Summer 1958

Right, top: Running along the single-line section near Henstridge, the first station south of Templecombe, BR Class 9F 2-10-0 No. 92220 *Evening Star* heads the 9.03am train from Bristol to Bournemouth.
28th September 1963

Evening Star at Henstridge

Right, below: Later the same day *Evening Star* returns northwards with the 3.40pm from Bournemouth. Pausing at Henstridge, the train has just crossed the boundary from Dorset into Somerset which lay about $\frac{3}{4}$ mile south of the station.

28th September 1963

Class 3F 0-6-0T No. 47342 ambles northwards with a 'pick-up' goods for Templecombe, passing over the River Stour on the Sturminster Newton River Bridge (Bridge No. 171), about ½ mile north of the station.

9th October 1959

Into the Stour Valley

Southwards from Henstridge, the S&D next reached Stalbridge where the railway joined the valley of the meandering River Stour. Just north of Sturminster Newton, the next station, the line crossed the river – the first of four such crossings – on a lattice-girder bridge, bounded on both sides by brick-built 'flood arches'.

Silhouetted by the mid-morning sun, a summer Sunday working – the 9.45am Bournemouth to Bristol – regains speed after making a scheduled call at Sturminster Newton. This service avoided reversal at Templecombe; the next booked stop being Wincanton.

27th August 1961

No. 92220 *Evening Star* is featured again in these two views of the 3.40pm Bournemouth to Bristol Temple Meads and is seen *(above)*, drawing to a halt at Sturminster Newton. The unusual feature (the 'dip' in the platform) provided access for foot passengers to the ramp at the northern end of the 'down' platform, the siting of which was staggered to that on the 'up' side. In the yard, empty cattle wagons await use on the following Market Day. The signal box, seen at the far end of the 'up' platform, controlled the single line block sections – northwards to Stalbridge and southwards to Shillingstone.

1st September 1962

Sturminster Newton

For many years, the busy weekly cattle market at Sturminster Newton provided considerable traffic for the S&D. The goods yard, which lay on the 'down' side of the line, opposite the station, also served the local milk factory.

A few minutes later, *Evening Star* prepares to resume the journey northwards. In 1961 British Railways introduced a standard four-character train reporting system; the code '2B92' being used to identify local S&D passenger services running, in either direction, between Bristol or Bath (Green Park) and Bournemouth.

1st September 1962

Left, top: On summer Saturdays, the 3.40pm 'up' from Bournemouth (featured in the two previous pictures) was scheduled to cross the 'down' "Pines Express" at Stalbridge, where the latter was booked to wait for nine minutes. The 3.40pm 'up' conveyed a mail van to be transferred at Mangotsfield to a northbound postal service, and was the only train given priority over the "Pines". This train is seen here running in off the single line section from Stalbridge and gaining the 'down' loop, to pass non-stop through Sturminster Newton, behind Bulleid Pacific No. 34043 *Combe Martin*. The Western Region style headboard was carried occasionally but only during the last weeks of through working via the S&D line, although for a short period in 1953, a Southern Region style headboard had been used displaying the full title – "The Pines Express".

1st September 1962

Note: In his books, Ivo Peters always referred to the 3.40pm from Bournemouth as the "Up Mail". S&D men however, used this title to refer to the 9.28pm 'up' *freight* from Poole Yard, a service which, in latter years, ran as the 8.10pm. Just to complicate matters further, the GPO paid for the running of the 6.48pm 'up' from Bournemouth, so perhaps, officially, this should have been the train to have been known as the "Up Mail"!

Left, below: BR Class 4 2-6-4T No. 80067 pulls away from Shillingstone with the 5.30pm stopping train from Bournemouth to Templecombe. By this date the small goods yard was little used, and already the sidings were becoming overgrown. The BR Standard Class 4 tanks were late-comers to the S&D, arriving in 1963 for use on the three and four coach trains which proved more than adequate to meet traffic demands during the final, sad years of the line.

18th May 1964

The Stour Valley – Shillingstone to Stourpaine

Beyond Sturminster Newton the S&D re-crossed the River Stour at Fiddleford Mill. This section of the journey equalled, perhaps, the beauty of the countryside south of Bath, although of course it was, and remains, very different in character. Shillingstone station, three miles south of Sturminster Newton, was set amongst the water meadows on the opposite bank of the Stour to Iwerne Minster House which, in Edwardian times, welcomed visiting royalty. Hence the provision of a platform canopy to the main station building at Shillingstone, an adornment denied all other 'Dorset Central' stations, other than at Blandford.

At Gains Cross, a mile south of Shillingstone, the railway passed through a deep cutting spanned by a high three-arched bridge (No. 184 – Cliff Bridge). Norman Lockett 'captures' Ivo Peters, as they both photograph a BR Class 4 2-6-0 (the number of which neither Norman nor Ivo recorded!) heading northward through the attractive sand cutting, with the 1.10pm Bournemouth to Bath.

1st August 1960

After calling at Blandford Forum, northbound trains were faced with a difficult climb away from the station to reach Milldown. BR Class 5 No. 73052, in charge of the "Pines Express", has taken full advantage of the sweeping descent from the summit at Milldown and, near to Nutford Farm, reaches the foot of the down-grade on a section of the S&D which provided glorious views of the Dorset countryside.

1st August 1960

The Stour Valley – Stourpaine to Blandford

Left, top: Beyond Stourpaine & Durweston Halt, which closed to traffic in September 1956, the S&D passed under the A350 Shaftesbury to Blandford main road. Now began a long sweeping curve, as the single line climbed from the floor of the Stour Valley towards Blandford. BR Class 4 4-6-0 No. 75072 is running at speed with the 9.55am Bath to Bournemouth, at the start of the 1 in 80 gradient towards the summit at Milldown, ¾ mile north of Blandford Forum. Today, the trackbed is severed by the route of the Blandford by-pass.

1st August 1960

Left, below: BR Class 5 No. 73047 hurries along the single line south of Stourpaine with the summer Sundays 9.30am Bath to Bournemouth. This service remained very popular and, by the early 1960s, provided a 'day at the seaside' at a cost of 13s 9d (69p) for a second class day-return excursion ticket from Bath. (How times change!)

27th August 1961

Blandford Forum

After traversing 16 miles of single line from Templecombe No. 2 Junction, double track was regained at Blandford Forum. Blandford (the courtesy title 'Forum' was acquired in 1953 – an event which led to a corresponding change to the nameplates of SR 'West Country' class Pacific No. 34107), was the only town of any significance on the southern half of the S&D. The station was, as the result, more impressive and included a subway for passengers. For photographers, like Norman Lockett, the public footbridge which crossed the line at the northern end of the station, proved the ideal 'vantage point'.

BR Class 4 No. 75007 waiting to leave with a Bournemouth-Bath train, and watched by the signalman from his box, the rear of which was cantilevered over the line serving the goods shed. Beyond the box, at the far end of the station, an ex-GWR pannier tank (a type no stranger to other parts of Dorset, but which always seemed very 'out of place' on the S&D) can be seen, shunting the goods yard.

28th September 1963

Unfortunately, Norman Lockett's occasional visits to photograph the S&D in colour on the scenic section of the line between Blandford and Corfe Mullen, appear to have been frustrated by 'bad light'. Sadly, therefore, the few transparencies discovered to date are too dark to enable reproduction within these pages.

The Wimborne 'avoiding line' (or 'Western Loop', as originally known), was just under three miles in length, running from Corfe Mullen Crossing to join the ex-LSWR at Broadstone. Opened first to freight traffic in 1885, and to passenger traffic the following November, the single line loop – which became better known as the 'Corfe Mullen Cut-off' – avoided the reversal of S&D traffic at Wimborne. From Corfe Mullen, the cut-off climbed at 1 in 80, past a small halt – opened in 1928 and closed in 1956 – before descending through the grounds of Broadstone golf course to join what was once the LSWR main line from Southampton to Dorchester.

Left, top: With the pine trees casting shadows on a bright afternoon, BR Class 4 2-6-0 No. 76015, in charge of the 1.10pm Bournemouth to Bristol, heads through the sand cutting towards the summit of the 1 in 97 climb from Broadstone. Note the unusual position of the 'down distant' signal, placed wide of the lineside at the top of the embankment; thus providing better 'sighting' for the footplatemen of 'down' trains on the curved approach.

25th September 1963

Left, below: Ivatt Class 2MT 2-6-2T No. 41243, with the 12.23pm Templecombe to Bournemouth, drifts down the bank past the Broadstone 'down distant' signal. The foot crossing, provided for users of the golf course (the grounds of which were bisected by the S&D line), can be seen in the foreground. One of four of this class of locomotive delivered newly-built to Bath in 1949, No. 41243 and her 'sisters' proved very popular with S&D footplatemen.

25th September 1963

BR Class 5 No. 73054 pulls away from Broadstone with the 3.40pm Bournemouth-Bristol. The 'S&D proper' ended at the junction with the ex-LSWR just to the east of the station. The platforms to the right served the original main line from Southampton – via Wimborne – to Dorchester. Until 1874, S&D trains travelled this route to the terminus at Lower Hamworthy, on the shore of Poole Harbour. No. 73054 is seen departing from the 'up' platform serving the later, direct, route to Poole and is crossing over onto the original main line before swinging left onto the S&D single line leading towards Corfe Mullen.

18th April 1964

From Broadstone, S&D trains ran the final eight miles of their journey to Bournemouth over the rails of the former London & South Western Railway, passing through Poole, Parkstone and Branksome. These are amongst the locations which will feature prominently in *Southern Steam – South & West*; the next volume proposed in *The Norman Lockett Collection*. However, to complete our 'journey' from Bath, a few scenes are included overleaf – at Parkstone Bank and at Bournemouth West.

BR Class 5 No. 73002 climbs away from Parkstone station with a Weymouth-Bournemouth stopping train. Parkstone Bank – $1\frac{1}{4}$ miles of climbing at 1 in 60 for S&D 'down' trains – was a delightful setting; a combination of pine trees (for which the Bournemouth area is famous – and the 'rational' for the title of the S&D's "premier" train), and purple heather. It was a location much favoured by Ivo Peters, who can be seen by the lineside to the left of this scene.

3rd August 1964

Parkstone Bank

On a lovely sunny August morning, BR Class 4 4-6-0 No. 75072 drifts down the bank from Branksome with the 12.55am Bournemouth West to Bath.

5th August 1963

It is evident from the large number of colour transparencies taken by Norman Lockett that this was a favourite location, especially during the last years of 'main line' steam. Yet, despite such a wealth of material, David and I have been unable to find a *single transparency* which portrays an S&D train! This shot does at least contain some coaching stock which, we believe, was berthed awaiting a return to the north, via the S&D. The locomotive featured represents a class which, from the 1950s, saw regular service between Bath and Bournemouth. Here, however, SR Pacific No. 34011 *Tavistock* is seen arriving with a train from Waterloo.

Summer 1959

Bournemouth West

The 'classic' view of Bournemouth West. BR Class 4 2-6-4T No. 80081 is busy berthing empty stock, whilst a modified SR Pacific waits to leave with an express for Waterloo. Today, this scene is transformed (for the worst!). Part of the station site lies under the A35 by-pass – the 'Wessex Way', whilst the remainder serves, inevitably, as a car park. Only the Midland Hotel stands as a reminder of days when S&D trains conveyed thousands from the Midlands and the North to their annual holiday at Bournemouth. Indeed, the Bournemouth of today owes much to the S&D of yesteryear.

2nd August 1964

The Branch – Evercreech to Highbridge

As mentioned in the Introduction, Norman Lockett appears to have paid little attention to the 'Branch' from Evercreech Junction to Highbridge until the final years of traffic over what was, until the opening of the 'Bath Extension' in 1874, the original main line of the Somerset & Dorset Railway. There are some interesting views dating back to the 1930s, but these were of course taken in monochrome and must wait to feature, perhaps, in some future volume of *The Norman Lockett Collection*.

Like most enthusiasts, Norman found the Bath to Evercreech Junction section of the S&D a far greater attraction, and who can really blame him; for there was no comparison between the variety of motive power which pottered across the Somerset Levels and that to be seen battling over the Mendip Hills on a summer Saturday!

Ex-GWR 0-6-0 No. 3210 draws forward from the middle siding at Evercreech Junction, prior to setting back into the 'up' platform to form an afternoon service to Highbridge.

24th September 1963

From Evercreech Junction, the single-line branch to Highbridge headed westwards, passing 'Elbow Corner' – the first of many isolated crossings, each with attendant cottage built to accommodate the crossing-keeper. Two miles from 'the Junction', the first station was reached, serving the village of Pylle. Now the line descended on a steep gradient through Pylle Woods and passed over two further crossings at Cock Mill and Stean Bow before reaching West Pennard station.

West Pennard

Right, top: As a wintry sun breaks through the storm clouds, No. 3206 sets off from West Pennard with the 2.20pm from Highbridge. The line towards Glastonbury is seen running dead straight into the distance; very different to the continuous curvature of the 'Bath Extension'.

3rd November 1962

Right, below: One week earlier, the same service – the 2.20pm Highbridge to Templecombe – was hauled by No. 2277, running onto the loop controlled by the attractive signal box at West Pennard.

27th October 1962

Glastonbury

Until 1951, Glastonbury was the junction for the short branch line to Wells. By far the most imposing station on the 'Branch', Glastonbury could even boast a covered footbridge – the only such example on the S&D. Right up to the latter days before closure, the goods yard remained busy.

The LCGB special – "The Somerset & Dorset Rail Tour", which featured earlier in this volume – also ran along the branch from Evercreech Junction to Highbridge and back. For this part of the tour the special was hauled by Collett 0-6-0 No. 3210, seen here about to set off from Glastonbury. The well-known landmark – Glastonbury Tor – can be seen in the background, just to the left of the locomotive's chimney.

30th September 1962

SHUNTING
BELL

10
11

By 1965 a single coach proved more than adequate to handle the diminishing numbers of passengers using the branch during the final years. Mirrored in the waters for the South Drain, a Collett 0-6-0 scuttles across the lonely Somerset Levels, passing Catcott Crossing – between Shapwick and Edington Burtle – with a train from Highbridge.

Near Catcott Crossing

Right, top: One of the best-remembered S&D railtours – organised by the Home Counties Railway Society – included a return trip along the branch behind two ex-S&D locomotives. The special is seen here, near Catcott, behind 4F class 0-6-0 No. 44558 and 7F class 2-8-0 No. 53807.

7th June 1964

Below: The LCGB farewell special also included a run over the branch to Highbridge and back. Ivatt 2-6-2T Nos 41307 and 41249 approach Catcott on the run up the line from Evercreech Junction.

5th March 1966

A Sad Farewell at Highbridge

Highbridge – where it all began with the opening of the Somerset Central Railway in 1854 and where, 112 years later, it all ended. Norman Lockett recorded, 'for posterity', this scene of Ivatt 2-6-2T Nos 41283 and 41249 after completing their final run with the last passenger train to be run over the branch.

6th March 1966

Dedication

Stean Bow Crossing. Typical of the isolated level crossings on the line from Evercreech Junction to Highbridge, and situated near the foot of Pylle Bank, about ¾ mile east of the station at West Pennard.

I wonder if those who still mourn the closure of the line ever give thought to the staff – like the crossing-keeper at Stean Bow – who lost so much more – a way of life? This book is therefore dedicated to all such men and women, who made it possible to enjoy a journey on that most lovely of railways – the 'Somerset & Dorset'.

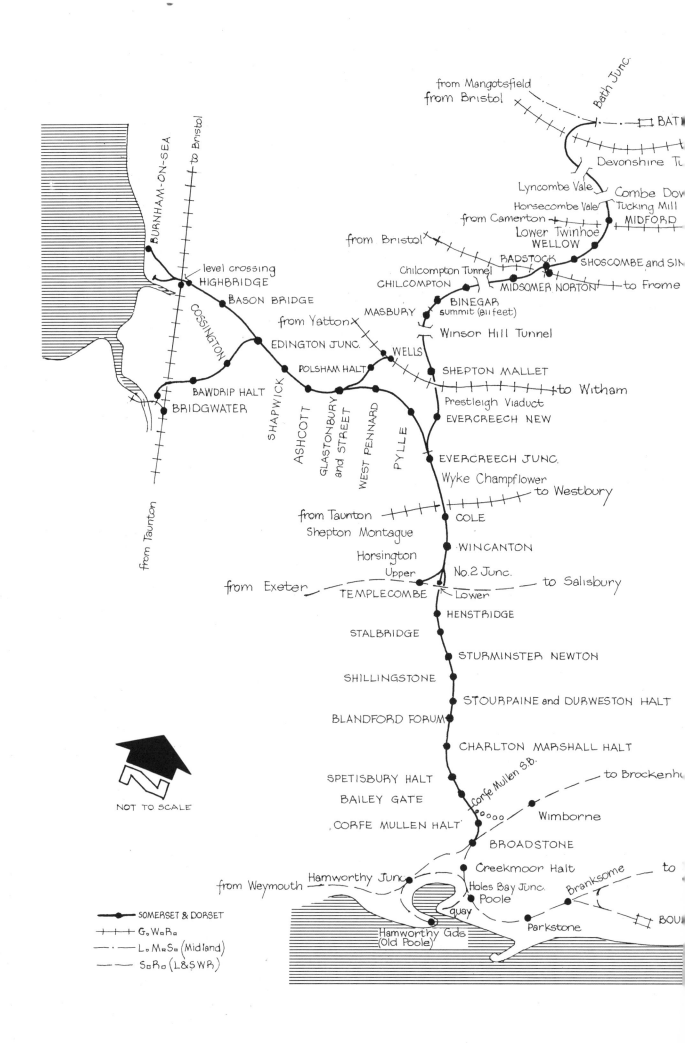

from Mangotsfield
from Bristol
Bath Junc.
BAT[H]
Devonshire Tu[nnel]
Lyncombe Vale
Combe Do[wn]
Horsecombe Vale
Tucking Mill
from Camerton
MIDFORD
Lower Twinhoe
WELLOW
from Bristol
BADSTOCK
SHOSCOMBE and SIN[GLE HILL]
Chilcompton Tunnel
CHILCOMPTON
MIDSOMER NORTON
to Frome
BINEGAR
summit (811 feet)
MASBURY
from Yatton
WELLS
Winsor Hill Tunnel
SHEPTON MALLET
EDINGTON JUNC.
POLSHAM HALT
to Witham
BURNHAM-ON-SEA
to Bristol
level crossing
HIGHBRIDGE
BASON BRIDGE
COSSINGTON
Prestleigh Viaduct
EVERCREECH NEW
BAWDRIP HALT
BRIDGWATER
SHAPWICK
ASHCOTT
GLASTONBURY and STREET
WEST PENNARD
PYLLE
EVERCREECH JUNC.
Wyke Champflower
to Westbury
from Taunton
COLE
Shepton Montague
WINCANTON
Horsington
from Exeter
Upper
No. 2 Junc.
to Salisbury
TEMPLECOMBE
Lower
HENSTRIDGE
STALBRIDGE
STURMINSTER NEWTON
SHILLINGSTONE
STOURPAINE and DURWESTON HALT
BLANDFORD FORUM
CHARLTON MARSHALL HALT
SPETISBURY HALT
Corfe Mullen S.B.
to Brockenh[urst]
BAILEY GATE
Wimborne
CORFE MULLEN HALT
BROADSTONE
Creekmoor Halt
from Weymouth
Hamworthy Junc.
Holes Bay Junc.
Branksome
to
Poole
quay
BOU[RNEMOUTH]
Hamworthy Gds
(Old Poole)
Parkstone

NOT TO SCALE

●——● SOMERSET & DORSET
+++ G.W.R.
—·— L.M.S. (Midland)
— — S.R. (L&SWR)